LOUDcracks/softHEARTS

by

Jean Lozoraitis

South End Press
Boston

Copyright © 1979 by Jean Lozoraitis
First Edition
Library of Congress Catalog Card Number: 79-63806
ISBN: 0-89608-069-2 paper
ISBN: 0-89608-070-6 cloth

Photos by permission of Sue Dorfman
and Michael Wingfield.

South End Press
Box 68, Astor Station
Boston, MA 02123
Printed at Maple Vail, U.S.A.
Typesetting and layout at South End Press

Table of Contents

Photo Credits

Photos pages x and 39 by Sue Dorfman
Photo page 6 by Michael Wingfield
All other photos by Jean Lozoraitis

PREFACE

I am no one's rival.
My feelings are gifts,
    not goods.
If you want to share
    my poetry,
you must respect my soul,
my womansvoice.

INTRODUCTION

i know my strength will be tested all
my life. i hope i will always be surrounded
by strong women..poor ones who work in factories
who are 50 yrs. old and black and say: yes, jeanie,
i know you could make it if you were black..
poor ones who are lesbians and know the dangers..
old ones who are poor and not so slow and quiet
with warmth still strong in their pocked bodies.
women who care to join in. i live for no regrets
because favors are like tax returns and welfare
checks, count on something you don't even have.
cryin for another break —what if i said there
isn't going to be one? if you like life, it
goes by fast; if you don't, it's gonna be a drag,
a prison that invites suicide..the tone of the
book is emergency; it is my voice. the object
of the book is to continue; may this happen to
my readers..may women continue with their
poetry -it, too, is my voice.

jean lozoraitis
worcester, mass.

I.
1967-1973

In the Lunchroom

The Factory

a woman walks away from her machine
squeezes a cigarette between two lips
and looks out the window.
a crow perches on a telephone wire
this is an omen for the rest of the day.

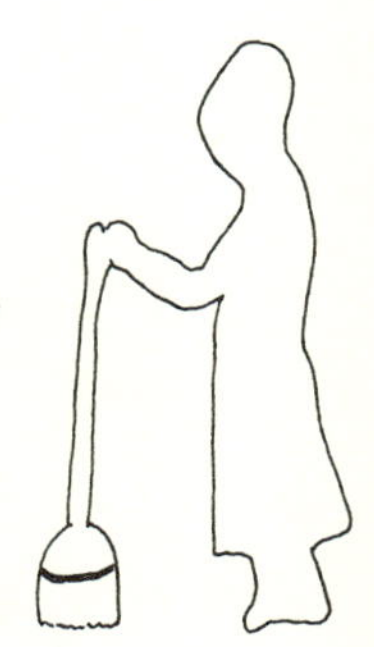

later, she counts the piecework tickets
stashed in her apron pocket
and urges the new girl to hurry.
she sweeps the dust with short strokes.
the new girl coughs.
the whistle blows.
there is alot to be gotten used to.

1967
brownshoe
don't rock
the boat..
what the women
don't know
won't hurt them.

puerto rican shore

the road was strewn
w/ rotten coconut shells
leafy plants grew
on one side.
a thick cement wall
guarded its own age..

Reaching the ocean,
i breathed in warm air.
2 little boys caught
crabs while their parents
kissed   on the other side
of the rocks.
i asked how they caught crabs
in the dark, they said
their hands were their eyes.

sharks were seen in the clear
water, by light from the hotel.

waves splashed higher
bathing me in drops of warm

1970

<u>on the tracks</u>

53 cars halt traffic
bend everything in their wind,
the station man waits for
the gloved hand to grab the mail
then disappear back
into the side window.

some boys hide in the bushes,
waiting for their pennies to be squished
on the tracks. they run out, throw coal
at Atlantic & Pacific, spit manly phlegm
from between their teeth.

Inside passengers dream
they were back
in Connecticut
last Sunday.

1970

JARRELL'S TRUCK STOP

Black
oil
men
pump fuel
bleached
out
women
watch
with binoculars.
discounts, smells
drones, jargons.
cowboys in trucks
riden em down
red snakes from Richmond.

1971

FIGHTING FOR MY LIFE EVERY INCH OF THE WAY

I am a pioneer
I am my children's
ancestor.

The dance
I step
will carry on
with soul-breathed songs.

Return to the fields
goddesses and gods,
entertain
sorrow and majesty
when we are born.

Then legends
like rivers
will flow
again.

The spirit of life
will have a new home.
And I will not
be sad
and oppressed
by an enemy
who sucks breath from babies' mouths.

1972

Tony Gomez, a beach near Provincetown

The Sun

nothing left to lose.
pills 'n arrows
kill for hell
SOMETHING FREE'S
wiped out;
with curse
and pain
of children's tears —
these odds
can make
a woman fear/some
times.

nothing left to choose.
Back to bloodsisters,
squeeze wrists
against the earth.
And love —
yourselves is growth
plants, bellies
Warm and Close.

nothing's left.
We won.

Our loves will join us to the sun

Our friends won't have to die so young —

1972

People who
pick out parts
in the revolution —
when we aren't
controlling ourselves,
we're trying
to control
each other.

10/72

Menstruation or
Keeping My Vigil of Rotten Fruit on Cotton

I am sickwoman
cramps haunt
my belly..
muscle-tite body
shivering
waiting
for blood
to run
thick and free...

1972

"It is a feudal attitude that attaches
importance to men and slights women..."   mao tse tung

part 1

capitalism makes
          women silly
          men mean
kills both
          poisons food
makes   rent high
drugs available and
          war necessary

                    part 2

                    amerika numbs/sickens
                    to death..
                    bleaches love
                    drugs to calm
                    fades pain
                    to quick memory
                    rots
                    to 30 or 50
                    then removes you

part 3

Amerika....
Land of take one to afford the other.

                              1972

MIDDLE CLASS LAMENT

1978

Don't ever let them claim it went unsaid
The strong ones making change, they'd rather dead
The world is owned by men with no respect for life
We trained for war, let's train for peace —
what else can we live for?
  chorus

Beware all folk who shy from social call
This lovely land of ours is going to fall
The breadlines will be long
The banks all locked and chained
We will be cold until we learn
but our freedom we'll have gained.
  chorus

It doesn't make a difference anymore
They got my head a hangin' to the floor
But I am not alone
There's others beside me
who choose to spend their lifetime
fighting poor economy.
chorus

16 congress, '72

i
am convicted
evicted
before i begin
working
to make good
from nothing.
my home hangs
CONDEMNED
baby where do i go now?
i have no africa
        to return to...

1972

can he sleep w/
both of us,
we not feel
jealous?
(sex w/o love
          is lonely)
this man this
opposite pole ——
(how many i
          counted
          mounted
          and compared,

                              1972

1st of my ego-boosting poems

I am the neworld
powerful
beautiful
breastwarm
and happy.
century-age
wind soothes
my skin
cloudspowder
rainsoil.

I ride the sun/blind
the earth: where love
pours when I shine.

Warming the
frozenuniverse
lighting creation,
I am a
goddessformation!

1972

i go in the laundry the kids pour soap all over me
 -like a shower, put lipstick all over my face -see? it's
a good thing the cops didn't come by..
        i get everything i want free. i don't need
nothing. this house is cold..
who's this, sally? i'll show ya how to draw. See?
that's good, honey. and i get crazy and i pick fights
with goddam bitches. yur beautiful, dearie. i gotta go
home. henry probably locked me out, dam bastard,
and i feel soo tired. give me a glass of water, honey.
        my father, god bless his soul, died, he drowned.
his last words were 'i'll make it up to you, baby.'
        i had a nervous breakdown when i was 15 yrs.
old -see this scar? it's from a mastoid. i was in a cell
for 5 days and the goddam window was broken and
snow was coming in. they treated me rotten, dirty
bastards.

IRENE. chew slower, yur gonna choke. want some
water? here's a sandwich in a baggie. u can save it
for later. it's starting to leak   here's another baggie.
how's your social worker? she didn't even hug or kiss
you when she came up. we'll walk home with you:
IRENE GOODNITE. IRENE GOODNITE. GOOD-
NITE IRENE, GOODNITE, IRENE, I'LL SEE YOU
IN MY DREAMS..

1972

the educated lady

to say yr mind is in a hole
wouldn't compliment another —
but my soul's in my hole,
so yr heart's in the right place —
except for the question of money,
which doesn't make it
when it comes to human life.
Besides, two cadillacs are hard to drive
and a pool will never be a beach.

i know u r suffering;
maybe my hands can reach yr whole.

                                    1972

*I mailed this poem to her instead of the ten
dollars I owed. Shortly, I received another bill in
the mail. This one was for $25.00 !*

MOTHER DIED TODAY

She walks in dreams
like nothing..
is a ghost
is a lover
in a locket.

She was everyday
now
once-in-a-while
very close at heart.

Memories wring out
dry up
to a plot
where the only lap
is a stone

or a couch
where 2 eyes
stared
passed me
scared me

screaming
live
gasping

nothing now
but white
men-flowers-cousins
and a smell
that chills my love.

1972

Anneke Dilsey Becker, Toronto

I looked myself
over today
and saw:
an infinite no. of angels
on the head of a pin,
painter and model,
music
and audience,
mother and baby..
man, woman
     and God
     I saw myself.

                    1972

<u>i almost was whore</u>

today
walking in bar
w/ drive between
my legs looking
w/ desperate eyes
at man who
would not
know my name..
some crazy spirit
teased me
to think
the fuck
would settle
the urge.

hole is
not just hole.
the blood
is my own -
my power
to destroy
shivers
to be used.

10/16/73
red baron

Spirit Life

my
anger
is a result of discontent
it is not bad
like the anger
of the oppressor -

it is raw change,
defying social gravity
becoming of free will
encouraging my spirit
to create life.
it is both personal and political -
my deepest emotions
remain enslaved.

my
anger
is alive
to burn or warm,
its power creates a way
for me to survive

and the struggle will continue
til the fear dies in the flame.

11/73

The Fire

i still see
the infinite patterns
on trees in the woods
    (tho the house is gone)
the lake of little islands
and laurel bushes
    (tho the well is filled
        w/ rubbish)
swings of vines
and teaberry plants,
cats —lost and wild
    (tho the hay is burnt
        to a crisp)
wild dogs in the barn
eggs to hatch, herb tea
broom toothpicks;
    (tho dumps and dirty books
        are there now)

eternal fire smell
tortures the living/me
whose memory survives
loss of love, blood
tobacco
pictures of mummy/secrets
lost secrets of a dead race
covered w/ a charcoal film...
crying to be reborn in me,
one of three survivors.

11/73

Birthday thot

goodness must seep
to the roots,
not force-fed

>   what i learned
from my wounds
that the sun
comes to dry..

1973

II.

1974

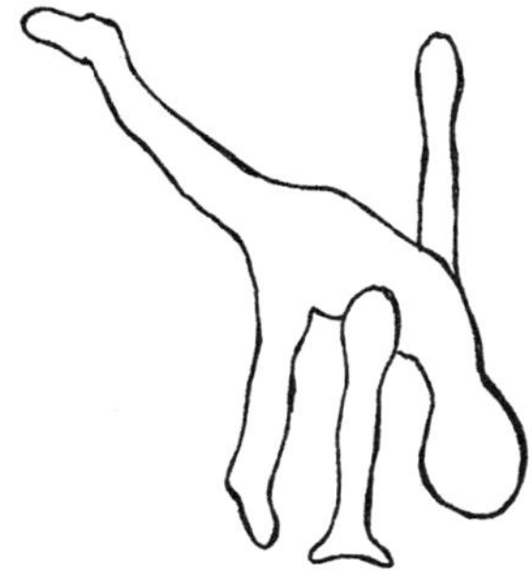

on the farm

HEARTPRAYER

Love in a wooden bucket
deep in a well
strong to carry
hard to tell..
water for thirst
courage to feed,
willing to face
the patience
to bleed.

3/23/74
3am

i am so good
i
automatically
make people strong/
i am so kind,
people want
to make gifts
but i must give &
take only in the
rite spirit/
the one with no regrets
or whys —
just smiles
and surprise.
i am so beautiful
that
my pain
may even
disappear
one day.

                                1974

memorial

women are always trying
to make men closer

women are dying to
make men closer

wo-memory
wo-memorial

to sumthing that weren't
even born...

1974
dedicated to
the ghetto mystic

OTHER'S DAY

DO U WANT
MY MOTHERMORALITY
TO KEEP
YR. SANITY SAFE —
OR
DO U DESIRE
MY
LOVERS LIPS TO
THRILL U TO
ETERNITY...
TO SEDUCE ONE IS
TO GET THE OTHER
BUILT-IN-mOTHER
FOR
ANYSIZECHILD!

1974

Common Theme

his hand travels
up the blouse;
twitching the tit -fast
circles
round the nipple; more
kiss and a hand reaches
r e s p e c t i v e l y
on the bellyforasecond
then
groping thru the juice,
making her pants loose —
he quickly
unzips   inserts
sometimes she cums;
counting the days w/ her
fingers on his back —
sometimes she doesn't
cuz he cums too quick —

and u see
how we use each other
and lie..

7/12/74

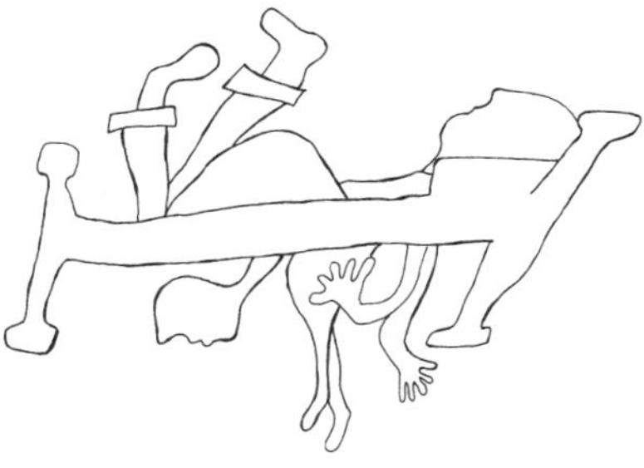

<u>patients</u>

go back home   go back home   everybody
keeps saying/ take yr pain
w/ u, i can only handle so much, u know.
go back   go back.   now that u've seen it,
settle down and let me tell people
u were a good memory.   aren't u glad
i told u things will get better?   what
more do u want!   i have my own problems..
it can't be that bad anyway..what is
wrong w/ u......

he cald again for the 2nd time and gave his name. he
wanted Judy and would breathe heavy when she
reached the phone; we told him he was being traced
but he laughed and said talk to me while i cum...then
tommy jumped out of the bushes looking like he'd
been in alaska-not shaved and wildeyed; bill drives up
w/ diddi at the side saying she'll puke if he makes
her suck his dick one more time. And nobody can
stand the heavies. makes them scared of sumthing
that won't grow anyhow...

stand up while u pray   put yr tray away; remove
yrself from the premises. not this semester, nope no
money -try another bank, maybe someone else will
think yr not a bad investment.

my wisdom teeth ache w/ knowledge
cocoons wrap themselves in tree
then be butterfly for a day.   it is
that short/ i'm saying we better
get our cocoons together b'fore the
rain..b'fore they cut us down and
burn us til we have no spring   no home

go back u cannot live w/ me.   we are separated
individually. i have no need.   yes u r crazy we can
help u..we will shoot u up don't deny u like it after
all massachusetts is one of the higher paying states
for wel-fear. get married   get married   just get out
of the way..we have no way to deal w/ u; though we
cannot give u what u ask for becuz u don't act like an
animal.   it is obvious u can take care of yrself, yr
hair is combed and u don't roll yr eyes......
maybe it was just an accident   it won't happen again....
go into retailing.   forget yr goals   things r always
changing in a society that is advancing so rapidly...
go back   think it over   see me next week.

1974
castle st. blues

i live in a jungle
my tribe is scattered and lost
the enemy plots our death, but
my guard is awake waiting
watching   learning secrets
to feed and protect me.

there is an evil spirit
in the jungle, i will learn
to be a witch   gather my powers to fight
for free territory -i will fight
blood with blood, it is my nature..
then celebrate the victory
with my ancestors...

1974

Shoptalk

sometimes fucking was
like a day in the
factory;
it was over
but what was it?

1974
the end of the day

"The Factory Girls"

there was marion who talked about the race riots
of hartsville, how at least southern whites called you
nigger to yr face. she asked me if the man i went
with was black..when i said yes, she said good.
marion wanted one of my poems to hang on her wall.

and the old white woman who wanted to crawl
in my sweater with me: it looked so homemade.

and viv who told me of shooting in her feet and
beating up a cop.

diana sagittarius blackwoman said how u had to
be hard and tough to use men. we talked about men,
money, travellin..'give me a dollar and i'll go
anywhere, cuz i know how to survive!' we kept each
other laughin..her husband's retiring t'moro from 22
yrs of service.

sally, they call mouse w/ alcohol breath, talked
with me about after 25 yrs, her husband asked for a
divorce — but she don't care a bit, 'I'm not looking
for any man rite now. maybe next year to help me
with my groceries, but i ain't looking for any man
rite now!'

and i listen to these women with pain stamped
on their faces: i make them my heroines, cuz they
make me strong.

edie and i once had a 3 part round of 'row yr
boat' goin, too..

and Joanne who defied the boss w/ me, who talks
about douche bags she buys from Zayres: she don't
like people who don't like black.

everybody resistin
while they're sittin
lookin for someplace
to go,
they give me hope for free.

7/29/74

Lesbian means:
fight
cut cops
give icecreamcones
and moviepasses..
fight the inevitable
as womn/means
any way u can
make it
w/o a man...

Since u were 12
no-ing there would
be no childrn/means
smiling when u pass
cuz we know
LESBIAN
is more than a haircut.

8/11/74

BURNED OUT

tonite sireens
and flight
from city walls
somewhere
echo
in our
back alley..
and families
in their
underwear
walk
Main St.
in drizzle
and night
find shelter
at Yur Place
clothes in a box
and memories in
ash on their face,
the face of a wino
from the rag factory...

FAULTY ELECTRICITY
BURNING CIGARETTE
We'll find the cause of
this damned thing yet.

DRINK HOT COFFEE
TELL US MORE
'bout the hooked man
fallin from the 7th floor.

HOW DID U KNOW IT?
WHAT DID U DO?
the place was full of junkies,
do u know if this is true..?

LET ME TAKE YUR PICTURE
FOR T'MORO NITE'S GAZETTE
this will be a feature,
it's the biggest fire yet —

burned up!
like hell!
rite across the street
(cheaper than a movie
and the feature never goes)
nobody knows
the cause.
the pain.

nobody knows
what it's like
to go insane/

will the sireens
come to my house,
knock on my door?

will they reach the middle
buzzer —
climb the 2nd floor?

take my baby
my sister   my friend
catch me sleeping..?

still-growth in the city
smell of burn for *days*
a list of never-nevers and
the pay-off never pays.

they are *all* on duty
watching us go down;

dying in the fires

burning desires
        like newspaper.....

1974

to the people
who died in the
fire at 728 Main:
Alex Shemeth
Olivine Gomes
Daniel Hampton
Walter Perkins
unidentified
Puerto Rican
woman in the
photograph

EN MEXICO -gto.

No hay luna esta noche
en San Miguel..se fue
a los estados unidos
para una oportunidad
mas grande..

No hay luna esta noche
en San Miguel..se derritió
y se cayó en un jardín
donde se convirtió
en un lirio
que un obrero trajo
al mercado para vender
por un peso..

No hay luna
esta noche;
uno de los niños
pensó que era una
pelota, la tomó
del cielo/ y todavía
se puede verla
rebotando
en las calles
despues del
atardecer..

There isn't a moon tonite
in San Miguel, it went
to the united states
for a greater opportunity..

There isn't a moon tonite
in San Miguel..it melted
and fell into a garden
where it became a lily
that a worker brought
to the market to sell
for a peso..

There isn't a moon
tonite;
one of the children
thought it was a ball,
snatched it from the sky/
and you can still see it
bouncing in the streets
after the sun sets..

1974

my 1st book=
    kiss on a railroad track
    red pimple on the
    middle of my big nose
    men staring at my padded bra
    someone asking me to dance
    before the others
    being in love every weekend
        proud cuz i said no
        scared cuz i'm different

the beginning of a book =
        losing weight
        eating good
        putting on
        mascara rite
        hating mummy cuz she
        waited til the last minute
        to tell me about periods
        and things
        going up her to get babies
        rolling my skirts up
        winning 1st prize for
        NEATEST NOTEBOOK

getting pushed down the corridor for big feet
        elected co-chairman for
        the sophmore bake sale
        sailing at 12 yrs old
        winning a dollar for my poetry
        and having ma hand me a bunch of
        rags for: my 1st period

taking drugs and then s'more
asking why til i burst
letting hair grow on my legs til
                    i don't care if they
                    snickerlaugh-
                    finding peace in
                    responsibility

the middle of a book =
     where i am now
     piecing all this valuable information
     together/learning
     how short time is/almost
     knowing how death feels
     memories linger   futures disappoint/living
     in a little box   reaching
     out for others in a
     most delicate way
     staying tough   thinking
     how hard it is
     to laugh myself silly

writing lovepoems to oceans
singing to plants,
correcting the false information
that i'm incomplete w/o a man
knowing where babies come from,
if i want one

the end of a book = dynamite
                    what an orgasm should be like
                    an accomplishment in love
                    knowing how to stop disease
                    not being afraid

is this what that freedmyth is all about?   changing:
                ways diapers wetclothes positions
                change in life wife tv stations
                for somebody else;
                going through them
                trying not to suffer
                dreaming on a ticket
                crying at the movies
                using motherpower,
                a straight-edge razor to keep alive

the next book = the unknown. the hour is late-u
                think-u should be home. cantakeit
                the nightmare   how much more
                being dirt poor
                a betterthanever life
                gifts for nuthin   trips to someplace
                gardens, treasures,
                soul-neverending

then the 3rd, the 4th book =
                a song for yr baby
                the quickness to kill
                a diploma to teach or
                a friendship that lasts

me. my book and i = something to give hope
                if u work in a factory or
                r the wife of a senator

not wanting to destroy myself
                is more than a lonely problem
                is nasty politics
                is 86 dollars a week is

finding things that will make me strong
                    will not burn unless i do
underneath all those words (GOING TO HELL BEING
UGLY LOOSE WOMAN STUPID GIRL SEXY
WITCH BABY BABY GOSSIP! TOO
INDEPENDENT NOT ADAPTABLE DOESN'T
BELONG HERE FRIGID)

          i know what i want
          if i can live past the opinions
          from doctorshusbandsbossesbrothers,
          even other women-
          that's when it hurts cuz
          ya know, we've all been made to feel
          like a cunt at one time or another

                              8/74
                    —*with all of my flowers
                    tryin to bloom, i'm
                    Somebody Special from
                    Somebody's Womb.*

III.

1975-1976

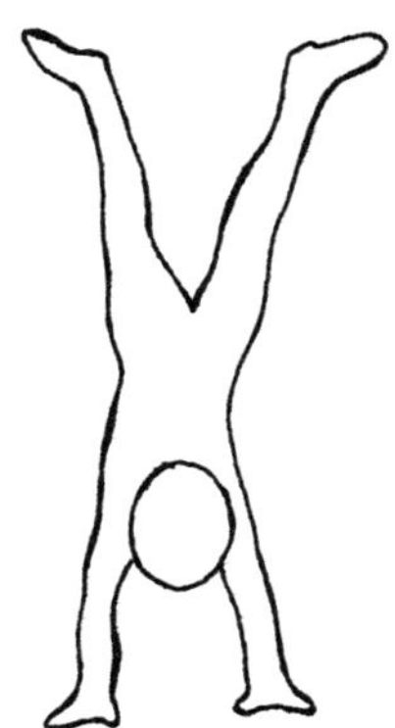

All Mayans Are Not In History Books

The world is full of
tiny island
shacks w/ the walls
so thin, father's farts
carry thru the house..
mothers w/ long black hair
sell basketfuls
of mango
on their heads.
children w/
nothing to do
play by the beach
in churning waves,

Baby has diarrhoea
on the kitchen floor
cocoa has flies
tortillas are
eaten plain.
full moon
shines thru the walls.

We study the ancestry
of these people
who should be treated as well.

1975

i love you/LET'S FUCK

have impressed you with my status
and taunted you with gold;
my knowledge is unbounding, say,
at what price will you be sold?
no, no you're not a prostitute
i love you for yourself—
then spread your legs and read my line,
i'll put you on my shelf!

SIR:

i hate to make a game of you,
or end up feeling bad
but i am tired and must go home,
a pleasant night i've had.
it doesn't have to end right here/
there'll be another day—
if you want to share your soul,
i'll find time to stay.

but i'm a busy woman
finding strength in woman-kind..
resistin' you usta make me blue,
but now brings peace of mind!

3/15/75
a mama carlotta's

While Fasting in Oxford w/ Alex

i am the queen
ann's lace in
the thistle -
catnip in
the stinging nettle/
and i alter your blood
w/ my power;
in chamomile
of the dump,
rose hip of the beach,
yarrow & clover
in the fields;
there is peace
in my kingdom —
sumac,
coney red/yellow
dock: all my
subjects defend
me against
human disease..
make me more
comfortable
in being myself.

1975

Mullein, farm road

rain in half/moon

buckwheat for
rheumatism/corn
for yr thigh;
shoulda listened to
the Indians
b'for we
let 'm die..

any special
symptoms: buy
aspirin from
the store/darvon from
yr doctor
and a note
from the surgeon
saying it is
necessary
to operate
on children
who don't know
any better..

that's US w/ a capital
livin condominium cave/
shoulda watched
the Indians
b'for we got
so brave.

shoulda known
ourselves much
better/
so brown ways
could mend
bones of
broken centuries/
peace
would come like
        spring...

shoulda listened
to the Indians...

1975
dedicated to Ben Harris

I AM IN LOVE

I am in love with
everywoman
because we are great.

We make cultures.
We make babies.
We make love.
We share
take care
　　　(and it's sad
　　　　　that sons kill)

We are the life
astronomers
have been looking for.

We are the bones
again and again
bearing
signs of space and race
　　　(no archaeologists
　　　　need apply).

1975

<u>to the little kids who
hav to make it w/ nuthun</u>

school
children
want to die/ take
pills for reality
be
junkie like
mother/ dream
airforce, chris-
miss, swat, tv..
*cross my heart
i'm goin
beyond
emergency
area and
into the
warm
of another..
rockin w/ rhythm
put 'm to sleep*

PILLTIME
take 9
then change
the subject cuz
they can't cope
bout 10 yr olds
takin dope —
and no breakfast
is the
only one
FREE!

11/24/75

The Circus

They came out.
16 Mexican princesses
climbing
the swing ladder
in time
to the music
taut young bellies
old round ones
extended in
circles overhead.

Then She approached-
The Mexican Queen!
Baring the leather
strap in her teeth
as they hoisted her
to the heights...
She crazed the audience
with her revolutions
while firecrackers
shot out of
a tinsel moon.

old tigers fought clowns w/ repetition
chased monkeys
bumped elephants
twisted snakes
prodded gorillas

$5.00 told the story
of the royal opportunity
to leave cracked earth
and dying mules
for roving tent life
and side show affair

16 princesses descended
the swinging ladders
while young boys
tasted brown skin
in their popcorn.

Mexican woman, agua azul

PROSPERO AÑO NUEVO

viviendo con nada
creyendo en nada,
encuentro en nada
un amor que
los que tienen algo
no pueden entender.

HAPPY NEW YEAR

living with nothing
believing in nothing
i find in nothing
a love that
those who have something
can't understand.

12/31/75

<u>what i thot about when he said i wasn't bubbly enuf</u>

<u>for him</u>

he
likes
bubbly
women. bubbles
women coming
out of bubbles..
Big ones, birth-
day cake and tub -
no trouble, mister,
bubbles will break
on u/yr dreams
will go down
the drain -yr
bath will turn
to champagne.
yr island wishes
will turn u to:
a husband doing dishes.
yr babies will make bubbles-
the fish u fry will look u
in the eye..

bubble pipes
bubble gum; why did
u have to
act so dumb!

1/22/76
'macropsychotic blues'

Magic Boriqua-herbs

found it
near river.
the mori vivi.
sensitive
plant/by
rain forest
and sides
of road:
roots for
tooth-ache.
ginger root
naranja leaves
crushed
and boiled
for yr needs/
stomach and
before you sleep.

malageta (maybe bay)
used in alcohol
for rubs and pain.
conderamor - yellow flower
diabetes cure.
Celantrillo-sprout
then plant, use
similar to parsley.
Mavi bark
for beverage —

y hierba para la vaca
para nada.

1976
To:
Doña Maria
tito y caballo
Carmen y Nandy
Cessie America
Ester y Debby
almendras, mares
bravos, fruta
arroz, discos/chinas
isla del mono;
historias
del pasado..
y dominos.

"family"

the man said he would build a neworld
      the woman waited
      she watchd/scratchd
      her fat belly and saw
the man, using tools and machines
      the fat belly emptied
      into a baby.
the man grew at using his tools -became
in demand and left to build other people's worlds.
      woman and baby watchd
the man dance with his friends.
      they watchd: the
      sun get orange
      time go by,
      birds, other babies
      sometimes they sung.

6/19/76

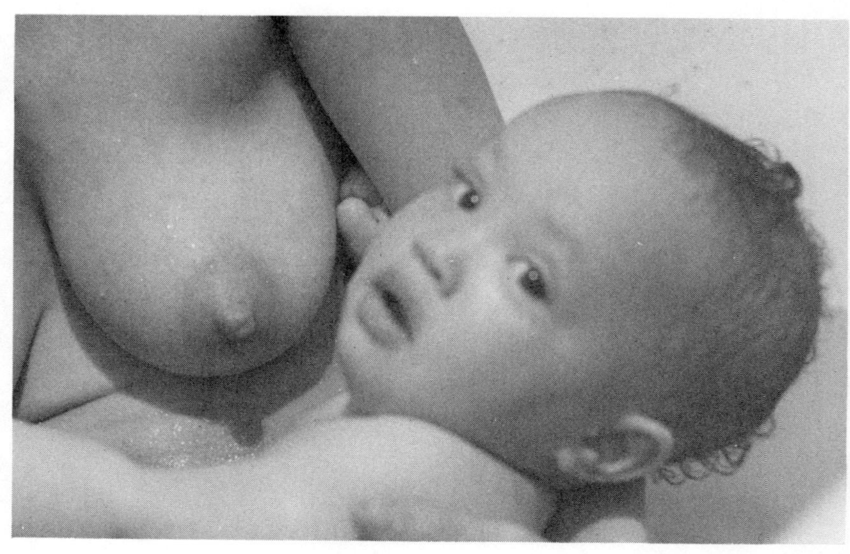

To Mrs. J.

mayor of castle st.
smokin   scoldin
old woman
who fed meat
to my dog..
up many-a-summersnite
hackin   coughin
like nobody's business -
stumblin home
a week-nite or
2, w/ a beer
a word or 2..
glasses, short black
hair, city council
regular.
(Mat went too
bout a yr. ago -
left a race horse
and a parking space)
Mrs. J. didn't have
a car -
saw her snoozin
in the basement apt
the whole place,
a seamstress' nightmare..
talkin bout old times
curin her daughter's ills
(does big jim whose
teeth clack know..
Mr. M. on his bicycle..?)
castle st.   dead end
usta be a girl's dormitory
for a school on the hill,
that usta be a castle..
Big names
little people
hard times,
Mrs. J.
sittin on the steps,
watchin the garden grow.

1976

COOKIES, amerika *loves* its
cookies; in the middle of
all this poison floats a
dollar bill/sign that
amerika's citizens are
dying of chemicals
made for food and
bombs alike...the
ones in food are slow
to kill, and can make you
cancer or crazy..

NOBODY can relax,
there's too much
going on..the pizza
is grumbling, the coke
is too strong. the
cigarette's waning
rite into the lungs -
carcass of dead meat
made the menu at Lum's.

there's some terrible deals
beating all hands, no. 3
colored oranges, 10 sandwich
meat brands — w/ sodium
bicarbonate diffusing it all,
tell me, what are we *really*
preserving!?

12/7/76
nite of j. jordan/e. knight

IV.

1977-1978

1970

2. I got a head and a body does the same thing as you
Now I found me a way and my fist's comin' through
Don't you mess with my land cuz my passion is through

3. Now don't you take off your hat cuz I don't like your head
You got somethin' inside but it needs to be fed
Too bad we can't be equal people instead.

4. You can talk all you want, you can scream all your might
But don't fuck me over cuz I'm just gonna fight
You keep sayin' you love me but I know that ain't right.

The End

BITTER, i feel
so bitter,
you didn't earn
me tonite...
my head was into
how i should
treat people
better/ it was into
being pissed at
Jacqueline for
comparing me
to the catholic church-
it was all
downhill
from there—
and when u
started singing
sexist songs
and lovin' it,
my mind was
nowhere near..
so i
SUFFERED IN SILENCE
too yin. must have
been the
two coffees
and having so
few friends.
i envisioned
pushing the car
door open, and
falling to the

road/ how easy
that one knock
would be/ how
hard for you
to ask me:
"What's wrong?"
i keep saying,
(maybe that's why)
fierce battler
am i, cannot be
freedom w/ needles
sticking into me,
knowing all i do
about injustice—
going through a
life w/ so much
pain—
closing my mouth
on demand/
relinquishing my
spirit—
ending up w/
bitter midnite
tears and
no one to understand
me alone
destined to
making things beautiful..

1977

*"it's not only hard to write,
but very hard to live."*

Fascism, American-style

Nite-lites reflect bars
on my wall/doesn't seem
to end, one category of pain
after another..it's not natural
somewhere along the way
we lost it, this long-term happiness.
now we pay alot/crosses to bear
nothing but bitterness to live on. lov
is the only thing that will save/
not charity, doin one good deed —
but knowing misery, waitin in its
heavy for the sun to come out..
a blue's song, where rhythm came out
of a prayer..it's madness..boredom
spit-fire anger that you gotta control;
watching the authorities
capture your soul, empty your pockets
making sure you're no threat
to capitalism: that teaches
welfare is a dirty word -fills kids
with rape, murder, Mr. Nice-Cop on tv
so when he comes to the Valley to shoot
black and spanish, you can say:
'how-do-you-do' while he go bang.

no more black or spanish disturbing
the police, i mean peace —which
nobody seems to find unless

they live on Salisbury St.
where the noise gets absorbed
by thick lawns. the owners of downtown
count their money while blinking city lites
stare on —
come! make more money
off despicable welfare checks,
drugstore flunkies
supermarket robbery,
fixin up ghettos for the rich -
tennis courts in the middle
of starvation/ may the hungry ones
eat your balls.

as for me, i'll get used
to hell/nothing new
no reason to leave;
all my beliefs, strength
washed up — i'm just sittin here
waiting to see if
they're really gonna make
Washington D.C. white
by 1980; we really gonna be
using nuclear power for energy;
do Tampax really have a chemical
that extracts more blood/

will this emptiness i feel
ever go away

will the dogs stop barking
in my neighborhood;

11/5/77
3:30 am

The Dead Wino

some said murder,
others cirrhosis—
papers said:
unidentified. did yur
geese w/ wounded neck
watch
as the shit got
beat out of you—
did the cats run
to tell yur city council,
brother, talk about
not having a chance/
talk about Christmas,
weather   anything
but old Bill's bones—
no fire to keep you warm;
were yur feet really tied
in a bag, yur money belt
gone/
Bill, did the dogs run
and hide; or was it
the cold   the wine
and it's still a social crime
that you had to die alone.

12/7/77

The Inheritance

I. Haying

the burnt house sat in the middle of field-
4 new farmers were beginning a summer
of work on this land.
horses were borrowed
machines were haggled over before bought

the hay came down with speed,
once experience was gained with the animals
and the mower.
Flies, lifting heavy harness and sweat
began and ended each long day
the 15 cut acres were now raked into rows.
foxes were seen playing at the wood's edge,
catching mice in the short grass..
starlite and clear skies guided the farmers' work

a neighbor was called in to bale.
the days now passed loading and unloading
a truck with hay to be stored for the winter
with the last nite, the last bale, came
the first drop of rain.
Excitement won over sore muscles
beer was drunk in celebration

II.Plowing

mist crowded out the sun, sky and day,
leaving only green grass to be turned over

by plow and farmer.
the earth gave up treasures that it hoarded
from years of no use
a snake, turned from its home, searched
the brown furrow for another.

a man came to spread his lime
on the fields, then they were disked.
rye seed was sown by handfuls-
once again the land was disked.
rains soaked the seed, starting growth
for the next year.

III. Leaving

fall looked close on the calendar
2 of the young farmers, confident
in their success of a season's work,
took to the highway for a visit west.
the 3rd farmer went to the city
for employment and friends
the last farmer stayed a bit longer-
there was still a little seed to sow,
a tractor to repair, tools to be collected..

someday the farmers would not have to leave.
there would be a barn and a house-it would
be bigger than the one sitting in the middle
of field, pa's house. pa.
He would be proud to know his children
would not abandon the place,
that it would serve as a dream-come-true.

8/25/78

<u>Me</u>

I.
Hidden
in a palm
my world waits
for someone
to hold it.

II.
Smooth,
sparkley stone —
smashing illusions
when thrown.

III.
each word i speak
aches in my mouth
taking with it
the sorrow from my heart.

5/18/78

Inner City

little kids, fallen
from their nests/ live
in cardboard boxes.

V.

Seagulls
unstaggered by
the wind, hurry
formation bound.

past midnite

dead branches hang —
   memories
      not quite forgotten

6/16/78

I.
passion,
heavy, mellow round;
i am
half sleepy
half wondering
what is to become of me-
Late nites..keep going
early morn..getting up
i am
at one end or the other

II.
tropical nov. air/port lites
turn my emptiness
inside-out
rain for the
next 24 hrs...   gutter water
                  gets to the sea

III.
surviving
can't believe
I'm doing it
(it's so easy to die)
me, woman, pushing hard
make paradise talk
force nothing but force
breathe lite
into heavenly bodies.

IV.
i cannot stop
it's too late —liberty
rang in my ears,
a motion was made
my eyes were
sentenced
to beauty.

1978

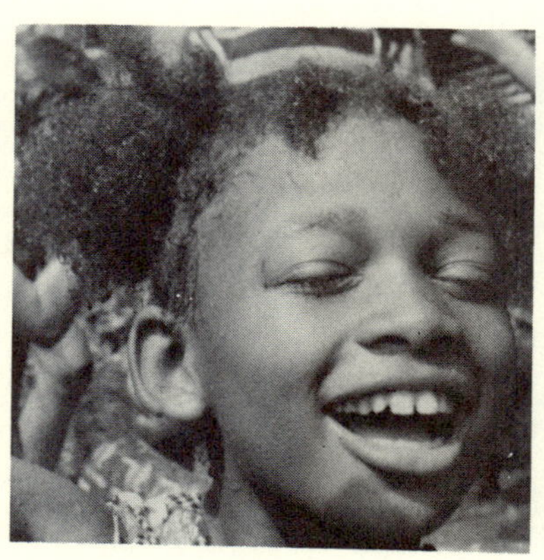

V.

From Me and My Sisters

Earth-Mother

I am a mountain.
You call me earth-mother
because I renew myself.
I stand alone and
nourish my children.

* * * * *

We speak of the Applachians torn
apart and left bleeding
by men's power-need.
We speak of the exhausted fields
bearing year after year,
pushed to the limits
by men's greed
But when a man alone feels weak
he lays down by the river
and seeks renewal from the hills.

* * * * *

You call me earth-mother.
And I refuse the name.

12/75
Barbara Mosberg

Grande Mal

I

there are minor deaths
exercises in blank:
the neural flash point
spilling over
into experience one walks in on
like bad neighbors -
soon enough to be embarrassed
too late to comprehend.

II
this is heritage -
a flap flap flap
on the floor.

C. Quicksilver

The snake has no choice but to shed his skin.
It was mine to let the rapist in.

I am innocent
I banish yr face from smiling
I banish yr mouth from touching
I curse you deaf, dumb and blind.

You have a hole where yr guts should be
The hole has little people surrounding the edge
They shout back and forth across the gaping sinew
The voices echoing throughout.
The hole is pitch black purple and veined with blood
It goes as deep as thunder.
They are yr unborn children.
Sometimes they scream. Sometimes they gurgle in
    shame.
They never join hands.
They just grip the edge of the whole as if they were
    falling in.
You think the rumbling in yr belly is from lack of food.

I almost denied my courage the right to speak and end
    this rape.
A primitive mother let it come through and save me
Mama, mameetee, auntie, grandma, nana, tata, titi,
    omee, sesute, mi abuela, mama, mama, mama
They were wailing and crooning for you to stop.
Their shins were bleeding.
The combs from their fingertip whispers could not pry
    you loose.

I came home wanting to sing.
Maybe I will hum again.

October 4/1978
susan lozoraitis

79

Sarne Stills, a block party on Piedmont St.

A Special Kind of Courage

A special kind of courage
kept inside yourself,
I really think you have it,
I really think you can try.

A special kind of courage
makes you sad sometimes,
but I think you can clear it up-in a while
even if you don't try.

A special kind of courage,
hard and bold and brave..
you got to try your best
in order to get your way.

A special kind of courage
deep inside yourself.
I really think you have it.
I really think you can try.

A special kind of courage
makes you sad sometime,
but I think you can clear it up-in a while
even if you don't try.

A special kind of courage
hard and tough and brave.
You got to try your best
in order to get your way.

1978
song by
Sarne Stills

81

The Insoluable

old eva-
    much fat
russian 19 yrs.
    factory-worker
finger-stubs
    eaten by machines
rheumatism:
('i got everything
    i don't like')
throwing
    bread-bits and
pieces of banana
to birds half-frightened
see-
    she tells me-
they can't talk
    but they
    KNOW-
they say they
    don't want
    to die

1969
Diane O'Flynn

A QUOTE FROM JEANNETTE

'..i want the best or nuthin'..
so here i sit,
w/ nuthin..'

5/22/74

<u>FROM: me and my sisters</u>

To the friends
who think of us
only to the point
that it doesn't
break their illusions!

GOODBYE.

SOUTH END PRESS TITLES

Curious Courtship of Women's Liberation and Socialism *Batya Weinbaum*
Theatre for the 98% *Maxine Klein*
Unorthodox Marxism *Michael Albert & Robin Hahnel*
Conversations in Maine *James &Grace Lee Boggs, Freddy & Lyman Paine*
Strike! *Jeremy Brecher*
Between Labor and Capital *edited by Pat Walker*
Ba Ye Zwa *Judy Seidman*
No Nukes!: Everyone's Guide to Nuclear Power *Anna Gyorgy & Friends*
Science and Liberation *edited by Rita Arditti, Pat Brennan, & Steve Cavrak*
Science, Technology and Marxism *Stanley Aronowitz*
European Communism in the 70s *edited by David Plotke & Carl Boggs Jr.*
Crisis in the Working Class *John McDermott*
Social and Sexual Revolution *Bertell Ollman*
They Should Have Served That Cup of Coffee:
   Radicals Remember the Sixties *Dick Cluster*
Slice the Dreammaker's Throat *Bill Thompson*
Ecology and Politics *Andre Gorz*
The Pentagon-CIA Archipelago *Noam Chomsky & Ed Herman*
Women and Revolution *edited by Lydia Sargent*
What's Wrong With the U.S. Economy? *Institute for Labor Education*
Indignant Heart: A Black Worker's Journal *Charles Denby (Matthew Ward)*

ABOUT SOUTH END PRESS

South End Press is committed to publishing books which can aid people's day-to-day struggles to control their own lives.

Our primary emphasis is on the United States—its political and economic systems, its history and its culture—and on strategies for its transformation.

We aim to reach a broad audience through a balanced offering of books of all kinds—fiction and non-fiction, theoretical and cultural, for all ages and in all styles and formats.

South End Press, Box 68, Astor Station, Boston, MA 02123